THE KITCHEN-DWELLER'S TESTIMONY

THE KITCHEN-DWELLER'S TESTIMONY

Ladan Osman

Foreword by Kwame Dawes

University of Nebraska Press / Lincoln

Acknowledgments for the use of copyrighted
material appear on page xvii, which constitutes
an extension of the copyright page.

This volume is published in association
with the African Poetry Book Fund.

The African Poetry Series has been
made possible through the generosity
of philanthropists Laura and Robert
F. X. Sillerman, whose contributions
have facilitated the establishment and
operation of the African Poetry
Book Fund.

Library of Congress Cataloging-
in-Publication Data

Osman, Ladan.
[Poems. Selections]
The kitchen-dweller's testimony / Ladan
Osman; foreword by Kwame Dawes.
pages   cm.—(African poetry book)
ISBN 978-0-8032-6686-5 (paperback: alk. paper)
ISBN 978-0-8032-7857-8 (epub)
ISBN 978-0-8032-7858-5 (mobi)
ISBN 978-0-8032-7859-2 (pdf)
I. Title.
PS3615.S53A6 2015
811'.6—dc23
2014041573

Set in Garamond Premier by Lindsey Auten.

For my family

CONTENTS

FOREWORD

Kwame Dawes

In her poem "Unsolicited Witness" Ladan Osman moves from witness, from someone simply observing, to a strange and surprising participant. This complicity is not without danger, but it is also marked by a belief in magic even in the face of the most ordinary and base things: "newspapers and dog shit."

Osman's management of syntax is deft, controlled, and it opens us to a kind of soothing music. It is because of this that her surprising observations and her tough, unsettling questions become both comforting and madly disquieting. This man, this shower of frogs, this abuser of Barbies, this ankle-grabbing monster seems harmless enough, and yet, by the end of the poem, we are left concerned about the speaker. We encounter this figure again and again throughout the collection—the "brother" and the "one-I-should-call-brother" (understood quickly not as a biographical personage in the poet's life, but as a mythic construct that is still rooted in the poet's experience of gender), almost two sides of the same figure of pleasure and danger. This is the magic brother who will go on adventures with the speaker of these poems, and it is also the brother who says in the poem "First Red Dress," when he sees her feeling giddy with her body and loose summery clothes:

"Go out in that dress
and you'll get split like a watermelon. Down there."

He becomes then, in that moment, one of the recurring figures in these poems—a figure of the imagination, of exaggeration and of tough reality, what her aunts call, in the poem "Admonitions," "bad men in the bushes." These are the shadows of danger that haunt all of Osman's poetry. Her persona speaks as a child fully aware of the dangers that women face—drunk white men shouting, "We'll catch you," men whom she is drawn to look back on even though she knows, as she says, there is a connection between these men and the girls who are "tossed into ravines and stuffed under bushes" ("Twigs").

The "kitchen" of the Kitchen-Dweller is full of creative possibilities but equally full of dangerous things: fires, knives, and poisons.

For all her willful playfulness, the thing that reveals the wonderful range, and what I call the anchoring of Osman, is her splendid management of sentiment even while she is dealing with difficult and emotionally fraught subjects. In her poem describing the moment a father discovers he is diabetic and the moment the daughter finds out as well, the narrative is rich with precise and evocative detail, the dialogue is elegantly trimmed to the symbolic, the essential, if you will, and finally, Osman shows us that she understands how to complicate situation and emotion with a capacity for physical detail in the cinematic sense and beyond—things a cinema can't offer us easily, physical texture and scent:

"Don't leave me," he said. "Don't tell your mother."
We sat on the bathroom floor, by the door and sink,
a space bigger than the coffee table. He smelled
like lemon skins, hot bread, moist sugar in its tub.
("My Father Drops His Larynx")

How achingly beautiful, how transgressively honest! Of course, the poem is, in some ways, about not obeying the second request: she does not leave him, but she tells, not just the mother, but everyone. In telling, she remains the "unsolicited witness," and yet what she tells and how she tells it does not feel like a betrayal.

Osman writes about relationships with disarming and sometimes painful candor. Tellingly, the work is never maudlin or pitiable. Her personae are tough, thinking women who want to face their own weaknesses and their own complicities in love and hurt head on. But they will throw a punch, and above all, they have the capacity to shout "Wow!" like the angry mother in the poem "Women Brewing," to hold in the fire and pray for the stillborn, like her grandmother, or, as the speaker says of herself, to think deeply, make sweetly honeyed tea, and talk. The poems are full of all of these impulses, and one has the sense that they are all necessary impulses and, beautifully, metaphors for the process and purpose of making poems. In a single moment of vulnerability in love, we see here a distinct sensuality, an emotional intelligence and humor—quiet, genuine humor:

The brew is a woman lifting her skirt
for a man who's seen what's beneath.
He makes no distinction
between her and stewed carrots.
("Diviner of Teacups")

Osman's poetics involve a distinctive willingness to allow leaps and non sequiturs to turn into arresting and engaging music. To have us follow her on this path, she has to win the reader's trust that she has some inclination about where she is going. This trust eventually comes from the anchors she employs even as she travels. One is the persistent and dogged desire to leave no questions unasked and to regard experience as worthy of probing in search of meaning. The second is her belief in poetry's capacity to transform through witnessing somehow, or to bring delight even in the face of harsh familial, social, and political realities. The relationship to the poem is best understood as a believer's relationship to prayer, one characterized by a delight in the form of the prayer—its predictable and familiar shape—and an equal delight in the magic of petition, confessing, lamenting, pleading, and prophesying, and, of course, the presumption of the existence of an audience.

> Neither of us knows the best prayers,
> but we can pretend, we can let them strain
> in the back of our throats as melody.
> ("To Abel")

In "The Kitchen-Dweller Testifies" the prayer becomes everything it can possibly be and more. Here is the prayer as lyric poem without losing its spiritual force, its capacity for doubt, or its capacity for beauty:

> If I'm lying may a chaos carry me into an unknown land
> without rain or tree to shelter me from desertion.
> May my mouth move westwards and never return.
> May I die and find myself living in a meek woman's mouth:
> my territory: tip of tongue
> to fleshy palate, from inner cheek to inner cheek.
> I'll know her humming, how it strains her throat
> because she refuses to sing even a quiet note, even alone.
> How will I ever communicate my feeling to her?

Osman's desire to communicate is a great comfort to the reader. It does not lead to inanity, or even to a lack of complexity. Nor does it lead to poetry that is merely "accessible." Instead, what we are never in doubt about is her desire to find the language to express the difficult things. We trust this impulse in her, and because we believe it, we are willing to follow her into the miasma of thought, language, and, occasionally, discovery.

It is, these days, reassuring to be able to say of a younger contemporary poet that she is fiercely protective of women's rights, that she is acutely aware of the politics of race, and that she understands her Americanness through the complex prism of migration and the effects of war, and she is all of these things while writing poetry of studied craft and exuberant passion.

It is equally satisfying to say that these qualities alone do not represent the raison d'être of her writing—she writes out of a passion for language, out of a compelling pleasure and challenge in the potential of the voice to humanize us, or perhaps even better, to affirm our humanity. Osman is a warrior poet, and she is dangerous because she is especially gifted and disciplined about her craft, her technical facility with the poem. This collection offers numerous examples of this skillfulness, but two should suffice here. Her poem "Clearing the Land" opens with a provocative gambit—at once, the sensual and emotional and physical awake with potential violence:

Could be it happens when I take off my bra:
I'm convinced someone will take my heart.
An adult lament made my child-fear fantastic:
hand come clearing my chest like an old homestead

What follows are some twenty lines that range through the pleasures and anxieties of sexual discovery, of gender awareness, of emotional and physical exile, war, the complications of thought, and the limitations of language, and just when we are certain she has somehow lost her way, we observe the design of the poem—a design held together by her syntax and rhetorical grace. We return to the chest, to the vulnerability of the woman in a world in which men still have privilege. "My heart," she says, "is a mother who wants a farm":

A soap-smell rises with the heat of my chest,
lilies inviting a deer to gaze, briefly graze.
My heart is a mother who wants a farm. My body
the daughter who receives land from a man
she doesn't want as a lover. The land squats.
My heart's farm not offered but found sideways.
I need a little less of it. I won't use a tiller here.

Can't we look for green cardinals? They'll move
along the fence watching for mealworms
as we shake them loose from weeds.

Later, her poem "The Pilgrims" opens with a most memorable metaphor—a simply enviable line: "Something is pressing against the hymen of madness." She holds to its implications of deflowering, rape, loss of innocence, regret, and that strange complicity that we can find in the escape of madness. It is never the best form to quote a whole poem in the middle of a commentary, but I can find no better way to demonstrate Osman's bona fides as a lyric poet than to quote "The Pilgrims" in its entirety. It is a poem of profound chaos that moves with tidy sanity, which, in turn, allows us to travel through its complexity:

THE PILGRIMS
Something is pressing against the hymen of madness,
and the clouds blush where streetlights seek them out.
The wind tries to run but is my herald.
It circles the cat that buries what is present.

I undressed madness and cannot unwelcome
my lust for her.

When she comes we will bow against a sun
that regrets lighting our path.
If I look, I will not be able to see her
but when I reach out my hand I will feel her there
and her back will say, walk.

In the opening poem of this collection, "Silhouette," Osman asks a blunt question about her place in poetry—about her right to write poems. Given that the poem's note, "at a Claudia Rankine reading, University of Chicago, 2011," alludes to Rankine's outspokenness about race around statements and work by Tony Hoagland, one can well imagine that the question is a sincere one Osman hopes will be answered by the book.

> My voice is small as it asks,
> What will it matter to them if I make a book?
> I am one poet. Isn't there space for me?
> And the tears are sweet, completely sweet
> as if they mean, even now you don't believe?
> The colonizers couldn't have dreamed it,
> the preoccupation with the heights of my soul,
> my intangible qualities, if I am only the silhouette
> of a shadow. If this poet is white in third world countries,
> what am I here? It's possible I'm just like the wind in the curtains.
> They monopolize part of the eye.
> The wind makes its mischief in goose flesh.
> A girl closes the window.

"Isn't there space for me?" she asks. And at the end of the collection, there is another apparition, another figure threatening displacement, and Osman has returned to the troubling question of her place in poetry, as in life. It is "a large bird' that lands on her sill. She confronts the bird:

> "What do you want?
> Should I die so you can
> take this bed?"
> It looked sad and faced westwards,
> eyes jaundiced. So I sat up,
> and told it to *leave, leave*.
> I flapped my wrists.
> It turned from me, facing west.
> A breeze lifted a collar of feathers.
> I was again it, myself.
> By then I was ready to go crazy,

lay my head on the bottom of a tub
filled with my crazy.
And then it flew away
and the torsos and ocean went with it,
and I was myself, again
and peaceful with my three shadows
when walking in any new night.
("Western Gate")

The external force is tamed and sent away, but a more internal power lingers—that seductive madness that we have seen in "The Pilgrims" and in so many others of her poems. But that "crazy" flies away, too, leaving a different kind of "crazy": the "three shadows" that go walking. It is beautiful, for they are *her* "three shadows."

The most remarkable thing about this book of poems by Ladan Osman is that it all seems so effortlessly good, and it would seem as if she has accomplished something quite remarkable without breaking a sweat. No doubt she has worked very hard on these poems, and this may explain their "effortlessness." But this coolness, I venture, comes also from the surfeit of language that one can see in her. I have read this gathering of poems many times over, and every time I am finished, I am left with the sense that Osman has so much more to say, so much more to show of her lively, probing, and startling imagination. This is saying a lot, for as you read this book, you will recognize that even here, just here alone, she has a great deal to say and has said it beautifully. She's only just begun.

ACKNOWLEDGMENTS

Thanks to the editors of the following publications in which these poems, sometimes in different versions, first appeared:

The Account: "Apparition One," "Apparition Two"
American Life in Poetry: "Tonight" (column 336)
Apogee: "That Which Scatters and Breaks Apart," "Trouble"
Artful Dodge: "The Kitchen-Dweller's Interlude," "To the Angel of
    Accounts on a Holy Night"
Bat City Review: "Visitant," "Western Gate"
Broadsided: "The Glass Images"
The Feminist Wire: "For the Woman Whose Love Is a Bird of Passage,"
    "The Man Who Puts Dirt on His Head"
Fifth Wednesday: "Convoluted Mattress," "Proud Flesh"
Heard: "Words We Lost in the Water"
Kweli: "A Dove Sings for Young Lovers," "Silhouette," "To Abel"
MELUS: "The Albatross Holds a Note in Her Bill"
Narrative: "Connotation," "Desertion," "How to Make a Shadow,"
    "Ordinary Heaven," "Water," "Woman, Ego, Shadow"
The Normal School: "Amber Doll," "Gnats," "The Woman in the Field"
Poet Lore: "The Figures," "Women Brewing"
Prairie Schooner: "The Kitchen-Dweller Testifies," "Section 8,"
    "Situations Wanted"

RedLeaf Journal: "The Beetle," "Following the Horn's Call," "The Trumpet Testifies"
riverbabble: "Parable of the Leaf"
ROAR Magazine: "Diviner of Teacups," "Her House Is the Middle East"
Transition Magazine: "Denotation," "The Key," "My Father Drops His Larynx"
Vinyl: "Verse of Hairs," "Admonitions"
Waxwing: "First Red Dress," "Twigs," "Unsolicited Witness"

For their love and light: my family, my teachers, teaching partners, and students; Kwame Dawes, Matthew Shenoda, Chris Abani, the African Poetry Book Fund, its editors, and my siblings there; the University of Nebraska Press, Slapering Hol Press, the Michener Center for Writers' excellent staff, Round Top Poetry Festival, Storymoja Hay Festival, Chicago Arts Partnerships in Education; Ted Kooser, Roger Reeves, Fady Joudah, Van Jordan, Brigit Pegeen Kelly, Airea Matthews, Michael Adams, Donika Ross, Dean Young, Shamala Gallagher, Krista Franklin, avery r young, RJ Eldridge, Tina Fakhrid-Deen, Betty Bah, the Headley family, Mónica Jiménez, Barbara DeGenevieve, Greg Broseus, Suzanne Ashworth, Abhijat Joshi, Meta DuEwa Jones, Christopher Adejumo, Weléla Mar Kindred, Keith Wilson, Kenyatta Rogers, and Aricka Foreman.

I am grateful to the Michener Center for Writers through the University of Texas at Austin, the Cave Canem Foundation, the Fine Arts Work Center, and the Luminarts Cultural Foundation for their generous support of my work.

THE KITCHEN-DWELLER'S TESTIMONY

Silhouette

at a Claudia Rankine reading, University of Chicago, 2011

I enter: carpet, curtains,
large, framed pictures of robed white men,
a glassy glare over a forehead, below the voice box,
students in bland shades.
I don't belong, the luxury of thinking,
the wealth of talking about thought,
privilege of ease among important people.
I am afraid of them, their smell,
their cotton, their expensive running shoes,
their faces so hard to read
when they make odd-placed sighs
at black people histories. There is not one
bright color. A professor laughs—
quick, self-turning, a paper cut
to his own heart.
I hate myself for the shame of forgetting
the books on my shelf,
the many others read on the floors of libraries,
corners of bookstores where the cashier can't see me.
Shame when I see all the book spines there ever were,
their colors and textures like women bent in prayer on a high holy day.
My voice is small as it asks,
What will it matter to them if I make a book?
I am one poet. Isn't there space for me?
And the tears are sweet, completely sweet
as if they mean, even now you don't believe?
The colonizers couldn't have dreamed it,
the preoccupation with the heights of my soul,
my intangible qualities, if I am only the silhouette

of a shadow. If this poet is white in third world countries,
what am I here? It's possible I'm just like the wind in the curtains.
They monopolize part of the eye.
The wind makes its mischief in goose flesh.
A girl closes the window.

What living and buried speech is always vibrating here . . . . what howls restrained by decorum?
— Walt Whitman, "Song of Myself"

I

Ordinary Heaven

I arrange a doll in a chair and wait for her to speak.

I want to say, "Be!" but am an ordinary creation.
I watch for the folds under her eyes to twitch.

I have many dreams, I say to her.
In my dreams I'm better than myself.

I soften peppers in a well-greased pan and make announcements.
I say, in the afterlife we cannot allow a single particle of our light

to diminish. I am not a woman-prophet,
but I know paradise. I have seen my soul sitting on grass.

There, I learned God doesn't know shame, and after six days
He allowed our atmosphere to make certain souls wince;

we crawl under its magnificence. Here, I can attain ordinary heavens.
Here, I attend to my book of questions. What is love? Why does it say,

"Allow me to mogul your soul?" Where does it keep what it takes?
What does the prostrating shadow request? Why do rocks enslave

water? What is the slave's poem? Does the sea favor its roar or murmur?
The doll cannot answer. The furrow in her bottom lip suggests

that entry into ordinary heaven only requires recognition of it,
for the soul's arrogance to weigh less than a mustard seed.

I am sorry for you, I tell her.
You witness but don't testify.

Words We Lost in the Water

If Somali *hail* fell from the sky, it would be cardamom.
The sidewalks would release its scent under our heels, we would fill
burlap bags with it, odd grains of rice mingling in the tea.

There my father is the *Lion of God*
and not a man who talks about position,
not a man who remembers position.

There, lips smile for *love*
and *hope* sounds like the English *need*:
don't piss on my *need*, we say.

Trouble falls, a rock
down the narrow well of the throat.

Chest and *bullet* are twins
separated by a handsome jaw, a beauty mark.

There my brother is *Victorious*
and not the odd grain in the sieve of my father's heart.

Unsolicited Witness

I saw him change an *F* into a *B* by the lockers.
He caused the lines to curve.
He made bridges where there were none.

He was the one who poked a hole in the Barbie pool.
When the girls filled it, there were sudden tears on the old carpet,
all the dolls on their backs, expectant.

He used to wait under the basement stairs and grab ankles.
It was a monster, he'd say.
He helped his baby sister hide food by the water heater.
He swept the dried rice and cereal.
When their mother found all those fast meals, he stole a Sky Dancer
and propelled it into fluorescent bulbs. The shards came down as glitter.

This is the man who used to play in the dirty stream
where the Sears used to be.
He showed me the frogs.

I followed him to a magic dumpster filled with day-old pastries.
There were newspapers and dog shit inside.

To Abel

Sing your song sudden, let it be
a car door hitting the breastbone,
small tear in the pink of an eye.
Who hears it when you keep its hum
at the base of your throat?
I do.

I am the sister who watched a bird bury its dead
and did not understand.
You said "help," intimated "help" with a howl
that caught in your voice box.
But the dogs listened for it, and called to the ambulances
that took you after plans gone confused,
you alone on a stretcher
or between the cracking lines
of a parking spot.

Neither of us knows the best prayers,
but we can pretend, we can let them strain
in the back of our throats as melody.

Sugar

My mother bought a large bag
for my brother's return.
He likes his tea very sweet, she said.
He'll help me finish this bag.
He'll come by winter, she said.
This week, the terrible honey
of Callery pear trees, new mulch.
A new bag in the pantry.

Section 8

The afternoon me and Cuckoo find out it's not the name of our neighborhood, we laugh until we're drooling and choking on our spit. We roll on the floor until our mom calls us hyenas. Then things are not so funny. The free toys from Salvation Army are embarrassing because we're Muslim and anyway, Santa never comes to houses that don't have chimneys and real stockings, even though you left him milk and cookies warmed in the microwave. We were small and stupid. Now I hate the bulk food boxes we used to build Toytown, the garbage bag of Barbies and board games every winter, that I am not Andrew, whose parents come to school to talk about their jobs and give him money to buy 5, 6, 7 books at the book fair every month, that I have to write my parents are "separated" on the free lunch forms. I want to ruin something for someone. Over the fence I say to Halima: hey, you're poor, everyone here is poor. And Halima says, my backyard is nicer than yours. So what? I say. You got that patio set with welfare money so don't pretend. She looks sad and then I'm sorry. Later some big girls come to my door and say, we hear you're telling everyone we're poor, and I say, we are, we all are, and they say, how the hell do you know? Because my brother told me. They don't say anything because he's bigger than all of us. No one will walk around the block with me for a while. We don't look each other in the eye. Then we are back to double-rides and going halfsies on freezies from the corner store, and it doesn't matter that our parking lot is full of cars all day and night, and that everyone writes their parents are "separated" on the school papers when everyone's father is upstairs or outside doing God knows what.

The Key

I was under the kitchen table, guessing who was at the sink by how they used water when I heard my mother say to my father, what about this job, that one, those people, did they call? And my father said, everyone says no. I see all the doors but none of them will open. My mother said, maybe we just haven't found the right key, I'll go look for it. They laughed for a long time. Their toes looked at each other. Maybe they forgot the bag of keys in the crooked-mouth dresser. I lined up the keys on a windowsill, metal on metal on my fingers until they smelled like missing teeth. I looked at the best one: large cursive *F*, a scarlet ribbon tied to it. It had two teeth, like my baby sister. I tried the little door behind the community center. Then the big-kids door at my school. The shed of a house with a backyard so large the family could never see me. I got grass and sand and an ignorant pebble in my shoe. Dust climbed up my pants so I could spit-spell my name on my leg when resting. I went back to our neighborhood. There was a black cloud over it while the nice neighborhood down the hill shone. A girl said our house was darkest and the first raindrops fell on it because we're all going to hell. When I told my father he said it was "isolated" or "separated" storms. So it was true we were set apart for a punishment. The next day dozens of dead flying ants covered our patio. I took all the keys and tried all the doors in the abandoned mall. One unlocked. It was a room with white walls, floor, ceiling. White squares of wood flat or leaning in every corner. The door closed behind me and no key would work. Maybe the room would swallow me and I'd get invisible if I didn't stop screaming but then a surprised guy, white, wearing white, opened the door. I wanted to try one more time but my keys disappeared and everyone said they were never real.

First Red Dress

It's sleeveless, upper back bare but I'm eight
and not fleshy. Skinny and free to show skin.
I want perfect bows. I straighten
and am cowed, the knots too tight.
Try again, disappointed in the new wrinkles.

My mother's hands smell like lemon detergent,
her palms a little moist. It's August, my birthday month,
everyone's necks and backs of knees slick in the afternoon.
I run to show my brother, and the-one-I-must-call-brother.
"I like it," my brother says.
The other says, "Go out in that dress
and you'll get split like a watermelon. Down there."

I can twirl and balloon its full skirt.
I take full strides. How could I rip anything?
Fall on a big rock? Cut myself down there,
though it's never happened before.
First red dress and difficult to put on, take off.
Red cotton with peacock feathers all over.

I leave the bad feeling of the boys' room,
think of my flesh as a broken watermelon,
seeds making pupils on the feathers' eyespots.
Pink flesh and black eyes on my flesh,
like the time I dropped a melon on the front step
after carrying it alone from the car.
Me and my mother and brother ate it anyway,
spooned into its split. Left some for the ants.

Admonitions

I always kept my knees together, even when I washed myself.
I knew the story of Mary. The miracle conception.

Maybe I would walk too many times on the rusty railing out back
like a gymnast, like I was told not to.

My aunts said girls who weren't cut had dirty shames,
could get pregnant just like that, hennaed fingers snap.

"Niece," they'd say, kohl eyes kind. "Don't run so fast, don't walk too far.
Don't play outside after sunset.
There are bad men in the bushes. Only jinns go out when it's dark."

Twigs

The one girl who runs faster than me smokes twigs she collects
    from the playground:
this way, my mom can't smell the smoke. Do the ones that have
    buds on 'em, she says.
It'll get you high faster.

Two men.
Fat. Drunk.
White. Old.
Hey, girls. Come on, don't run. Don't run from us.
We'll catch you, wait 'til we get ya. Ha ha.

I can't stop myself from looking back.
There are girls tossed into ravines and stuffed under bushes.

Where to hide, where to hide as I run past the other girl, past the
    swing sets,
the playhouse where the older kids pee when they can't hold it.

Verse of Hairs

First, a chapter on the hammock a mother's skirt makes
for her daughters' heads at dusk on Sundays
after each has come out of her bath, thinner-skinned
and raw in the palms, smelling like the chlorine in tap water,
lotioned from head to toe because the rest of the week
they'll only do their faces and elbows and whatever is showing.
What is the smell around their ears? Wet cotton?
Clean asphalt drying in springtime sun?
The sunlight is scented when white clover
grows with grass. This is an old verse, the girls
like caterpillars falling out of trees when it's barely warm:
even the inside of a quiet cement mixer would have been better
than cool pavement. They come with hair dripping ornaments
on their pajama backs. What about a verse
for the dismay of one daughter cutting her own bangs
into a bald spot, the hair put in her top drawer,
a thousand hairs in underwear waistbands, gaps
in the wood. A mother might cry trying to put a tail or braid
where she can't. Or, the surprise of fungus on a scalp:
the ointments, the red comb set aside,
the hot water and Tide bath it must take after every use,
the tuft of hair left by a dermatologist's razor for yet another
sample, tufts of hair that fit no tail or braid. A mother
can cry trying. There must also be a line about finding
curly hairs in pantyhose, the runs the girls made using tights
as blonde hair. Flesh-colored tights. Not their flesh but sufficient
for bombshells frolicking in carpet water, an old mattress
made Jet Ski, fluorescent lights something like a music video
shoot. We must have a verse about the grease under a mother's
fingernails, how they become translucent after twisting two sets

of prickly rollers, their inserts so similar to caterpillar hairs
or a bottle's scrubbing brush. Also a passage for the little braids
or buds in the baby girl's hair, the hair that barely makes tail or braid.
A mother can cry.

My Father Drops His Larynx

My father just found out he had sugar in his blood.
I was eight and used to running from his footsteps.
The coffee table between us when he'd ask for cold drinks
because I'd spill the hot ones out of their saucers.
He'd ask me who really broke something, after the lineup
with all the children. He'd ask: "Was that decent?
Do you think you lost your dignity doing that?"
He smelled like lemons. He smelled like himself
despite aftershave, detergent. And like skin
after the repeated use of water, a vague musk
found in every house I knew, even the holy ones,
but only in the rooms near sinks. My father
had sugar in his blood so it made sense
that he was acting funny: all that sugar
and no tired gum to dip in it, give it new flavor.
I'd wait for the bus every morning eating sugar
right out of the container, feet in the kitchen sink
until I saw other children pass in front of the house.
Only the teeth seen when I smiled rotted.
They looked like concrete, gray and porous.
One morning, when my mother took my sister
to the daycare past the church, on the wrong way
to school, after my brother was already walking
with his friends, my father called for me.
He was not on the loveseat behind the coffee table.
And I was used to him coming out of his room for dinner,
used to the closed door of his small office, the room
that would have spared us from two bunk beds in ours.
He was on the bathroom floor, toilet seat up,
resting his temple on the rim. The bathroom
smelled like warm toilet water, like the seat left down

when the house was hot, like the Sprite-and-tap-water
drink I gave him when I took too many sips and had to hide it.
"Please help me," he said. He vomited water.
A hard white thing fell into the bowl, and I tried to stop him
from flushing. When he spoke, the sound was acid, a scab
picked too early, canker sore bit by accident over and over.
"Don't leave me," he said. "Don't tell your mother."
We sat on the bathroom floor, by the door and sink,
a space bigger than the coffee table. He smelled
like lemon skins, hot bread, moist sugar in its tub.

Denotation

He shows me his foot, the ash on his heel a delicate lace.
He measures the space between ankle and sole with his fingers:
"This is a nigger. If anyone ever calls you that,
knock their teeth out." I push up my pink glasses.
They slide down the sweaty bridge of my nose.

Connotation

Walk as God intended. Straight, even.
Not prostrating, a shadow.
And not too proud.
I have the complex my father warned against.

When the woman whose hair is like down spits near my shoe and says,
"This neighborhood has changed since these people came"
I can't say, "You are the spitter; you are the trash."

I'm the shadow prostrating.
Not the shadow as it lengthens,
water spilling from a heavy bucket.

Can you smell my scalp through my scarf?
Earth after water licks it.

Parable of the Leaf

Let us not strike each other, not even with a leaf of grass.

What about the woman whose body is solid as a tree trunk,
her old hands the branches that slap the tops and sides of city buses?
She hits her granddaughter once. Again. Another time.

The old woman doesn't scream anymore,
only whips her limbs about the girl's face, the soft parts of her ears,
the girl's dumb ears now the same color as her purple-brown lips.

The heart is so weak.
It doesn't matter if its beats skip
or rise to a soft space below the throat.

I dream of a baby left in a shopping cart under a box of cereal.
Even when he clings to me, I hesitate before his mother.
I am the weakest, the leaf that falls when there is no breeze.

How to Make a Shadow

Give her the spirit of a dog,
a black dog with a sword in her paws.
Tether her. Put Position
at the bottom of a well filled with rats;
rats with shining backs, their eyes shillings
in the pocket of a man who sweats,
sweats at the ass crack for Position.
Say to her, *bark* and she moans. Sudden chorus.
The grass sits up to listen and asks:
Who is the weed that will not sever?
Why won't the earth take water? Say, *bark*
and she bites the space between ankle and sole. Say, *no*,
to her. *Be quiet.* Like, may the seed stop up your throat.
Or, hold the sword between your teeth. Cut your tongue.
Say, *I nigger your heart, I eat your sleep.* I give you the dream
where you kneel and can't straighten.
Get down from here, into the well.
Fight the rat or let him ride like a disaster on your shoulders. Say, *no.*
Say, *don't open your mouth again.* Or try to open it
with a bridle there. I ride you when you're so small, small beast.
No.
It will ring as omen: smiling dead squirrel at the curb, shining scythe
    under a bus bench,
dead birds in a nest, dark feather under the doormat.
Black tongue, black roof of mouth, black paw pads, black nails,
    black snout, black spit.
Say, *die*, and she comes like a jinn,
silk shadow at your bedside:
I nigger your dreams,

bitter seed in the well of your throat. I will not scatter
from your heart. I grow a tree there.
I rest in its shadow.

Intangible Quality

We are not always yolk.
Sometimes we are the yellowed grease
on the side of the skillet,
running headlong into flame.

I enjoy watching men's eyes eat women like breakfast.
There is so much that passes
between thigh-meets-chair
and shine-in-pupil.

Is there anything that keeps what it takes?
I thought it was the heart. I hope
it's not the earth, the grain it issues.
Shoots touch skin and say, get away from here.

Is there any veil except time?
One of these days I'll take the light out of my eyes,
leave hollow globes.
I can make my voice birdsong in a graveyard

or hair between floorboards.
Hair mingled with carpet-scalp,
hair in the space between mirror
and frame.

See me.
Try to grasp me.
I make searching fingers
blister a man's mind.

Women Brewing

When my grandmother was mad she'd say nothing,
her fists curled, a cool element.

She'd swallow the fire, she'd drink it like it was too-hot tea.
She'd clasp her hands in her lap, hold them to her belly.

Cold mango calmed her, neighborhood gossip.
She'd pray for the stillborn.
When my mother was mad she'd scream *Wow!*
like a wailing kettle,

her Wow! climbing the stairs, floating down to the basement,
standing in front of open windows.

w o o o o o w! one time so loud and long
she ripped the stitches from her C-section.

Wow! from the kitchen
where she'd break the dishes.
When I'm mad I say nothing. I pace in the bedroom and think.
Soak my feet and think. Lie in the bed and think.

I stand over the teapot, wait until clove perfumes the house.
Before the kettle shakes, before it wails Wow!

I get out the honey. "Honey!" like the ladies on TV.
The kettle is off the too-red element.

The tea is not too hot. Not too hot.
Sugar dampens a boiling pot.

Honey, I say, drink some tea with me.
Honey, I say, let's talk.

Diviner of Teacups

The brew is a woman lifting her skirt
for a man who's seen what's beneath.
He makes no distinction
between her and stewed carrots.

There's one woman who serves tea to the second wife.
She varies clove and sugar but it's hard
to guess her meaning as she watches the other woman drink,
an amber band across her front teeth from all the good tea.

If she makes too little, it's worse
than loaning a thief the kettle
because she will never watch murky water
fall from its spout, leave a pebbled trail behind her.

When the tea bags sit too long or not long enough
her mattress will be lonely before her temples gray.
Did she want it to happen, or just watch,
a child who no longer responds to slaps?

The absence of cardamom or the taste of overused
cinnamon similar to the eyes of a girl whose father
upsets her and later lingers near a shelf of dolls,
unable to choose one.

The Kitchen-Dweller Presents Evidence

Proof of your Distraction fell out of your pockets.
A neighbor smoothed it out, placed it on a banister post.
Those sums flown out of your pockets, your insistence
on keeping the mail key to yourself.

I used to put your socks away first,
place your towel closest to the tub.
The best space for your everyday shoes,
a whole shelf for your dress shoes.

Do you know the stress of feeding a man
who goes with his belly full
to another woman's house?
One part our shared meal, then water,
the last part desire looking at the door.

We should invite Distraction here.
My father pronounces it "Destruction."
Distraction called God by her father's name
when praying as a girl. She still doesn't know why.
Oof, she even confuses her intentions.
She'll come chastened,
insist she didn't touch any of my things.
Destruction: she answers questions I didn't ask.

A call from Destruction in the middle of the night:
she says, "Get a drink, girl. I've got some things to tell you."
Well, at least he's not there. He's not here, so let's sleep.
Destruction never calls again.

Get under skin? Skin, you said?
I want to get the bone of your heart,
the marrow of your heart.
Here the sound of a hurt heart
is a man getting hit in the bathroom.

Know what it is to get your hair ripped out
in the tub you just cleaned?
I place that sound between your ribs,
a broken plate.

When I took those vowels, I meant every word I spoke.
I read you verse, and you told me my mouth transformed
in front of God and my mother. Now you are quietly
exhausted with me. Even your pupils are asleep.

Yes, I have been disgusting so much. I have kept
my good news to myself. Why aren't my vowels
enough anymore? When I recite to you,
I intend to get nervous and mess up.

Trouble

I have a chill in my womb.
I have a child in my wound.

Everything is massed up. The sea doesn't blow.
The wind rivers the sea in the wrong direction.

How will I get along with this man wolfing me?
How will I get alone? He herd me.

It never bordered me before,
what I got as a regard.

We used the hardest language.
We cast threats. We'll born in hell.

Some of us fall by the waistside
and some of us sore to the stars.

Her House Is the Middle East

There are so many spent rounds on the floor, and they sing like
    wind chimes.
Her husband stares at his family and thinks, what are these lesions?
Is this body my own?

Don't talk to her today. There is no resolution.
Only the unsaid. Rockets that come short.
Broken windows. Dimpled concrete.

The mistress' ghost is in the kitchen,
sticking to tile and baseboards, spiderwebs to grease.
"Do you know me?" the old sadness asks.

She ignores it and is a tank in a neighborhood
familiar with tanks. "Watch out," the people say
but their hearts don't beat faster.

That Which Scatters and Breaks Apart

Everywhere they turn, the walls ask, *why, why not.*
From every space someone calls a question
and there echoes so many answers, it's impossible to hear.

Save me, he calls.
Open me, she calls. *Divorce me.*
Their despair is a bird in an abandoned nest,
its brother has jumped out and died, its sister is dying beside it
and still it perches:
Do I fly?
Can I fly?

You're here because you said,
I hate you instead of *I'm sorry.*
You're here because you couldn't forgive
but kept on making stews and hand-washing his good socks,
blowing curses into hot water.

Invocation

Splay yourself on the floor, mop spread before God,
and may your submission remain false.
Let intention and the ground you stand on
crack and wander, become distant dimensions.
You crawled on my chest, a little spider.
You blended into bedding and startled me,
chipped my heart. May your own chest break.
I'll slap you into the floorboard, clean you up
with too much soap. Yes, I'll stand at that corner,
inhale and smile, remembering my frenzy.
We're beyond known curses.
You can still be ground meat in the street,
turned out by wheels, coiled under some car,
but I'd prefer you bleed on command.
May your stomach fall out. Since you like showing off,
drape it over shoulder, wear it to the market.
May your mouth let go of you. May it go to a place
whose light doesn't reach your fingernails.
Oh, I hope bad luck hog-ties you.
At least let it restrict your stride.
I hope the shadows underfoot stumble you.
I pray a snake grinds you in its mouth.
Not just bite, not just chew.
May all animals turn against you.
God, restrain my hands. Intercede.
My father is under my scarf if I don't beat you tonight.
My father, underground for a generation,
would never inhabit a hairline.
I'm going to beat you like I'm your mother.
I've got something sharp under my tongue,
some shard. Black metal in both mouths.
I'm fashioning a weapon.

The Kitchen-Dweller's Interlude

I will put into this bread a storm gathering water.
Do not take me, do not include me in this,
its plea a cat's purr, or a tree full of cicadas.

I will uproot your olive tree. I will smooth the bark or send
something to build a fungus like a small sun in its cavities.

What is the smell of trouble?
Love-trouble is poison on the roof of the mouth.
I want to have museum-trouble, the way the air changes
before someone cuts a portrait.

Into this bread I put the dog that runs after his owner's car, free as a horse.
Also a horse's tail trying to unbraid.
And a muzzle.

And the taste of gutter water. I stare dumbly at it.
Abase myself.
Is our love water I can't drink?

I blow a note into the hot oven, into the gap
between oven and countertop.

The Kitchen-Dweller Testifies

My husband has attempted murder with my own heart.
Percuss my chest and feel its resonance. Tap once, twice,
listen briefly with the palm of your hand, a fingertip.
I swear an oath, once, twice, thrice,
curse myself the fourth time.

Ask him about the night he told me he didn't know me,
and untangled me from himself like the tassels of an old shawl.
I tried to catch his nail, confuse his fingers.
Let him, too, swear an oath and open his chest so that we can see
the nights he speaks to me: *I waited, I missed you.*
Let him answer for the hand he put under my t-shirt
since the first days so he could feel me walking.
He must tell everyone here our story without confusion,
with every sentiment, in falsetto so everyone wonders if he's lying.

He described a wall reaching far into our past and once I saw it,
I couldn't climb it. I looked for a crack to wail into but there was none
so I wailed the way the least heartbroken woman at a funeral wails.
Then I wailed in earnest and chanted, *Warm, warm,* and packed
every good sweater I own in a duffel bag. I cursed myself
for leaving him without my papers and gold. How could I leave
without my two of my three wealths?

I swear he didn't follow me.
I didn't feel sorry embracing an airport toilet.
I offered my dreams as payment for three nights without response
    from God
and woke the fourth morning homicidal.

None can verify either testimony. There may have been a jinn
in the corner of the bathroom one dawn,
but I think it turned away from my commotion.

If I'm lying may a chaos carry me into an unknown land
without rain or tree to shelter me from desertion.
May my mouth move westwards and never return.
May I die and find myself living in a meek woman's mouth:
my territory: tip of tongue
to fleshy palate, from inner cheek to inner cheek.
I'll know her humming, how it strains her throat
because she refuses to sing even a quiet note, even alone.
How will I ever communicate my feeling to her?

Desertion

On earth I made men into mist, and now feel my own dust wander,
lift, and swirl. In the Afterlife, the weight of bodies
is heavy on the scale. If I were allowed to cry,
my tears would rust its beams. In the Afterlife, their weight
is a smoking fuse. Their souls don't extinguish, they ignite
and re-ignite and never explode. I wait.

They tamp bodies in the Afterlife.
They show me the razor's edge,
tell me to walk along it without looking down.
They make figures that stay at a distance.
I confront their backs.

I follow a man and his son
in a boat. They drift on shifting dune peaks.
They raise their shoulders against the wind.
I call to them, my voice a large dog in a crowded yard.

The Offended Tongue

If we are rocks in the desert,
who is the ice and what is the wind we accuse
of pointing us like a finger whose tip
curves back to its knuckle?

Which of our fathers is the water?
It must be a father. It's always a father
when a girl's shoes and her mother's shoes are put away
while the men arrange theirs like busy teeth at the front door.

If our mothers cannot be the wind,
I am the nailhead that waits for the corner of your eye
when you pass too close to a wall.

The words in the ridge of my tongue
are a woman who puts on her gold all at once.

When the Fire Is Not Enough

We watch our fire to its last embers,
damp chiffon flying out of hand,
out the car window. It dies fast
in wet branches, clacking its teeth
the whole time. The fire settles
into wood marrow, flushing,
flushing, turning sticks from each other,
to each other. We stir the fire, not looking
at anything in particular, knees northeast,
northwest. *Pioneers probably got so tired.*
"Of what?" *Of each other*, I almost said.
Of the ground. Dry grass in their boots.
My tongue hasn't felt clean for weeks.
I haven't scrubbed my neck for days.

The fire's liquid this time. I drop twigs into it,
like they're raw spaghetti hiding behind the pot.
"I'll eat you first," I say when food tries escape.
What's that joke about a white man's fire?
"The wrong size for conversation and sleep."
I was unsettled when you made it.

The fire is overtaken by other lights:
lanterns, strangers' fires,
animal eyes high off the ground,
even our small wet smiles in the dark.
Be smoke. At dusk over a red sun,
small, raw scar in the milky sky.
When the fire is not enough,
come in through nostrils. For years
I'll say, "Do you smell that?
I can't get that fire out of my mind."

Clearing the Land

Could be it happens when I take off my bra:
I'm convinced someone will take my heart.
An adult lament made my child-fear fantastic:
hand come clearing my chest like an old homestead,
the land left keening. No bush. No tree bearing fruit.
What shelter to keep wind from coming through?
Maybe the memory of stairs creaking behind me,
someone so close he must be holding my waist.
The sound of someone sneezing in the bathtub below,
or counting the red pulse of a smoke detector.
I need to talk to you so bad. Like farting
when I need to piss. In the playhouse
where all the children went when we couldn't hold it,
me and my best friend went to separate corners.
We showed each other our privates, gasped
that our meat was so same. That was there,
and we were girls, but maybe it can happen here.
I just need to ventilate. Don't the storms
make their argument multiple times a night?
I will repeat myself. Don't storms grow hot and strong
under sheets of water? Robins don't start talking
until 2 a.m. They can do the sweet work
as our ideas arrow to something. I'm in exile.
And you know about war. The stutter of war.
You've seen a people who have been difficultied.
Disastered. Dilemmaed. Are you late for an anointment?
A soap-smell rises with the heat of my chest,
lilies inviting a deer to gaze, briefly graze.
My heart is a mother who wants a farm. My body
the daughter who receives land from a man
she doesn't want as a lover. The land squats.

My heart's farm not offered but found sideways.
I need a little less of it. I won't use a tiller here.
Can't we look for green cardinals? They'll move
along the fence watching for mealworms
as we shake them loose from weeds.

Situations Wanted

Is there anyone who can be closer to me
than my forefingers?
My inner arm and rib?

I am looking for a man who will let me
make myself small then crawl
into his pocket as he watches TV.

He must know how to love his shadow,
how to say "I love you" to even the periphery
of his body.

Let us be wrists rubbing against each other.
I will pay you with good intentions.
I will be your friend, in the way mirrors befriend,

then grow water. But my face is a black mug.
You can drink its water and not know its bottom
until a bug bumps your lip.

If you are willing
let me show you how fingers know each other.
Even birds try to build their homes again and again.

The Figures

are all black in the picture I am drawing. I get sick of coloring them in.
My family. Girls I grew up with. A boy or two who would not look at me.

I do not fill you in with pencil or pen. You are
an outline. I love you.

I listen to your belly.
Sometimes it's a lake lapping against its bank.
Sometimes a small angry dog.
Or a woman screaming and billowing sounds as if she's in Hell.

I keep drawing, ink and silvery pencil smudges on my palms,
a callous on the heel of my left hand. I cannot draw right hands.

I give myself childhood bullies.
I make myself a little odd looking. A big space between my hair and
    eyebrows.
Everyone in my family is a version of my father except my mother.
I give myself her cheeks when I'm good, a peach-pit chin when angry.

Today you get a beard. There are times I don't remember
the color of your eyes
so I draw trees around you, so green, little buds.
Tomorrow gray and a little evil. The forecast in those eyes cloudy: a fight.

Money. Who cleans the bathroom most often.
Things people on TV say to each other.

There are nights when I count the tiny holes
from which chest hairs will come
and say, listening to your slow heartbeat,
do you ever think this isn't real?

Maybe I'm just drawing on cheap paper, living in my pictures.
I love you when you say, maybe. I'm glad you drew me.

Convoluted Mattress

If I build a fort around our bed,
the dining table chairs will be its outer walls.
The quilted pillows sent with a traveling woman, a courtyard.
The comforter cover with the blue flowers is the perfect canopy.
Under it we pretend we're at the base of a tree,
the type of tree that knocks on the window when it's raining hard,
its leaves shaking with laughter.

You hear the shimmy of our living room argument, the swish
of her thighs trapping her skirt.

If I reach out to you my palm will find the wrong place,
cold hand on your elbow instead of the fine hairs
on the small of your back.

I could ask you to be a seahorse with me,
our legs curled tails, our trumpeted noses calling to the surface.
Or we could roll toward each other,
over the small hill
our torsos have fashioned on the mattress.

Water

I came to you carrying water. I came to you
carrying silted water from a well,
muddied, carried in a bucket with a split lip.
My water tasted salty, and like the earth, and so
like blood, and I brought as much as I could carry
in a bucket that drooled tiny streams of water
on my mud-ashen legs.

In all our days together I have walked between well
and house enough so the path is marked
with the branching roads of my soles.
I have come to you so often the path has many other roads
if only you kneel in the dust and look for them.

I am subject to you in the way the water is subject
to the moon. You are subject to me in the way a wall
is subject to its roof. And like the water I expect
you to come upon me of a sudden, like flesh
out of a slit in cloth. And like the wall you expect
intimate collapses, capillaries of change
inscribed day by day on our surfaces.

I came to you with water from my deep well.
I came to you with earth for your ready water,
water in every crevice for the valley
that divides your tongue.
I held your head in my lap and traveled
the many roads leading out of that valley.

For the Woman Whose Love
Is a Bird of Passage

I am so poor before you. A grackle
whose colors are as good as a peacock's,
sometimes better in the full face of sun.
The love poem I meant to say

is lost. Instead, I swear an oath.
I curse like someone speaking
in a foreign language. Instead of *leave*

I say *scourge*. The proper word a chick's voice
still in its egg, a beak in a small crack.

Your blood is hot and flowing,
and the hinges of your heart's valves
allow traffic in all your heart's rooms.
Is that why the little kisses are not enough?

In your sigh there is the sound of water pouring
into a hot, empty kettle.

Let us have the same dream tonight, I say
and your smile is red glass in dim light.

I dream my front tooth is a crumbling pillar
and you are the entire city of sin, in collapse.
Instead of *leave*, you say *raze*. You are so poor
before me.

So let us paint the ocean instead.

We dip the brushes in a canvas that takes them
out of our hands. Now you are the grackle's tail
calling for eyes from the side of a road,
and I am the best room in your heart.

The Man Who Puts Dirt on His Head

I till you, my garden. I remove weeds
from you and only hesitate when the birds
share an especially sweet note. I wonder
if the lesser plants clinging to your earth
have a right to it. I pull arms from bases
when they reach out to a neighbor for help.
I observe the milk they produce when choked,
and deny them offspring. They used to have a right
to your earth, when you did not understand
how birdsong swells in the cathedral of a tree,
how a person can leave a life on the kitchen table,
how need is most powerful before dawn,
death's popular hour.

This dirt will not cool you. I remove
the weeds and leave the wildflower. I take
the excess and place it on my own head.
Who turns the earth? Who is the garden?
In the days when butterflies and beetles
escort us in our work, we are both water and wind,
seed and petal, farmer and the earth that resists,
relents. We remove the uninvited worms.
How their color reminds us of the private places,
how they cling to the roots of anything.

The Glass Images

1.

Oh TV. The things you tell me.
A man in a store taking enhancement pills
so he can expose himself to Barbie.
You don't tell me if she's the real Barbie
or the kind who's too big in the middle
and wears smudged lipstick.
The reporter thinks this man is funny,
but I can appreciate the effort,
the bravery it must take to see yourself.
I don't wear shorts for my husband.
I'm not used to showing myself.

2.

What happened to that polar bear, Zero?
He would not eat his food.
He would not climb onto his display rock.
I was so proud of him. It would be better to starve.
They needled him. Airlifted him back to the rock.
What will he do when he wakes up and sees
that he's back where he started?
Who will tell us if he's heartbroken?

3.

Do you remember the girls who snorted
the ashes of their roommate's father?
You show me the ridiculous with a straight face.
If I spend enough time with you
I can know something about people.

No one cares if those girls are haunted.
They are told to pay bills, past-due rent.
They are not ordered to sneeze out the ashes.
The judge should say: give a memory of her father.
Tell us something of the dead, of the living,
of what happens in the dark.

To the Angel of Accounts on a Holy Night

I have put grooves in the couch thinking how ugly people are getting.
It's me who's getting ugly.
Give all believers a place of rest in the Hellfire, I pray.
I mean to say Hereafter. I don't know what I mean.

If this life is a marketplace, and I am the vendor of my soul,
what have I been selling in a shop with sticky floors,
its bad fish smell migrating to tongue?
Overripe fruit, bruised and starting to leak.
Rice spilling from burlap. Milk coating plastic.

I am not the woman who sells shining pots,
ceramic dishes for burning scented coals,
and gold for every size of wrist and finger.

If the heart is the flesh that taints the body,
isn't mine the spiderwebbed meat of a spoiling apple?
Whose hand has sliced it open? Who is holding the knife?
Close the apple, I want to say to the Angel who takes Account.
Leave it. I am not ready for you tonight.
I am not ready any night.

Tonight

Tonight is a drunk man,
his dirty shirt.

There is no couple chatting by the recycling bins,
offering to help me unload my plastics.

There is not even the black and white cat
that balances elegantly on the lip of the dumpster.

There is only the smell of sour breath. Sweat on the collar of my shirt.
A water bottle rolling under a car.

Me in my too-small pajama pants
stacking juice jugs on neighbors' juice jugs.

I look to see if there is someone drinking on a balcony.
I tell myself I will wave.

Visitant

A white kitten mews just beyond the patio,

tosses its head beyond the parking lot. I dread it.
I bring tuna in a Styrofoam cup. It refuses.

I bring water and wait. Sweat collects in the lines
on my neck. Still it refuses and gestures until I come

to a hole under the fence between lot and road.
I can't follow. Ants bite my toes and between them,

and the tuna, too. It leads me back to my patio,
back to the fence. After an hour I'm nearly in tears

and thinking, I'll go inside and enjoy my tea
and refuse any kitten that returns. Then, a heron.

White, too. It's large next to Texas trucks. I think,
suppose it kills me. What an absurd way to die.

It stands on a leg. Opens its wings, noisy curtain.
The heron waits. I don't ask it not to speak

because what if it answers? Suppose it's here to
guide my soul under that hole? Who can argue

with a heron when it's eleven o'clock and still too hot?
It goes. The kitten doesn't return. I cry into my hands.

Tears collect between my fingers. I wait until a gray hour.
A few ants stay in the tuna. Others leave blisters on my feet.

The Pilgrims

Something is pressing against the hymen of madness,
and the clouds blush where streetlights seek them out.
The wind tries to run but is my herald.
It circles the cat that buries what is present.

I undressed madness and cannot unwelcome
my lust for her.

When she comes we will bow against a sun
that regrets lighting our path.
If I look, I will not be able to see her
but when I reach out my hand I will feel her there
and her back will say, walk.

Woman, Ego, Shadow

Now I go into a brown sleep,
and look for Myself.
The last time I tried to see her,
I dreamed a white cricket.
Its chirp was deafening.
It survived the fire and disappeared.
Who has taken Myself?
When she was with me, dream was a mug
with a chipped rim, concrete against the lip,
sand in the teeth.
We never swallowed the missing pieces.
She was firmly affixed on a path.
She drank boiling tea
and said, girl, girl, how come
I got so much middle luck?
Me and Myself are two flames,
following a line of gunpowder.
We race, combine, then extinguish.
Me and Myself are a tree's ashen roots
and the sidewalk that boxes us in.
Me and Myself are a dial tone ringing out into the street.
Me and Myself are a small house, poor but not mean.
She is the tall window that shows a bed and an open wardrobe.
I am the young man considering t-shirts and jerseys.
She is the woman who looks up at him from the street.
I am the rat that runs eager in the yard.
Me and Myself have been raping each other
for a long time. Myself prefers a boot on the back of my neck
so all the neighbors can see her try to make Me pray to the pavement.
Where has she packed her purse and gone off to this time?

She could never tell if she would take the train north or south
until she frowned and let it pass or sat by the window.
Myself used to hear everything wrong. She'd say,
them Gulf Coast men was bullied and harnessed by their bosses.
But then, the wrong music was better if it whistled from her.
She'd say, the wolves been biting just to taste.
Or, the caterpillars are denuding their homes.
A tree's privates are the loneliest place.
Myself burned her palm into my back.
When I turn to see if she's there, she goes.
I am looking for Myself!
If you fall asleep on the couch and see her,
tell her I have a knife
for the place between her shoulder blades.
Tell her I said, you lie so good, you make the ocean sweet.
Tell her I said, something's standing by my bedside and I know it ain't her.
Tell her my sleep is usually navy blue or even greening gold
and I want it browner than knees or butt cheeks.
Tell her something that tastes like tea with grit in it.
Tell her I put poison in the pot and intend to watch her drink it
while she's telling me something crazy. Tell her I'm out of breath.
Tell her there's a paw the weight of a large stone on my chest.
Tell her I've seen the moon come red out of blackness.
Tell her the sand is rising as one people and rushing somewhere.
Tell her she's missing all my wildness and if she doesn't come on soon,
I'll have to go looking for My Shadow, and Myself knows
Shadow's the kind who don't take her shoes off
for Nobody.

The Woman in the Field

A circle of children with hair the color of withered cornstalk
hold out batteries and say, put your tongue on them. Try it, try
while a woman looks on with milky eyes,
her hair husks in boiling water.

Gnats

I can't tell why I think the dried corncobs
in the gravel and the mattress under the tree
were not put here by children who bite so fast
they leave rows of kernels.

What does this mattress make me imagine?
What stalks this strange field? Who is eating my head?

Years ago, I would have imagined children jumping
off the branches, landing hard on the mattress,
shouting out when the odd spring caught a rib, an elbow.
There would be a young mother with a plate of corn,
red-faced from the heat and laughing.

Then, bird songs were not ominous.
Danger did not orbit like a gang of gnats.

Apparition One

White tiger in the snowy sandbox,
a concrete corner visible in lamplight.
It guards the alley to the bad boys'
house, the two who held their mother
hostage. The alley where dogs go crazy.
Every single one of them lunges for a face.
Every one turns to that single lamplight,
strains on tethers toward a far corner.

Apparition Two

We saw ghosts near the cat-shit sandbox.
We beckoned the girl-ghost once.
She wore white, rode a white bike
around the lamplight, in perfect loops.
The air around her looked like a video game
played in a lightning storm:
shredded newspaper, or dirty snow.
She would not ride her bike closer.

Amber Doll

I gutted you ten years ago, cut your limbs with a kitchen knife
and threw you in a dumpster across the street.
I watched the three-legged cat grieve you, head in his paws.

Amber, you dull-eyed monster, how did you find me?

You did not scream when I sliced the seam of your spine.
You stared. You smiled your dry-lip smile.
It was not me who colored you purple.
I did not keep you under the stairs.

But we never put rollers in your hair.
You were not even good enough for Brown Bear,
who the Paper Dolls would not give the time of day.
We could have let you marry him.

You are an ugly girl in a paisley dress got from a bin at the
    Salvation Army.
Your eyes roll white in their sockets, even though you're cheap,
and your eyes don't move when you're made to dance,
when a little sister is playing baby and rocking you in her arms.

Remember that night you were on top of the fridge, legs
    swinging?
I just came here for a Fudgsicle, I thought.
I threw you. Your body was fleshy,
your back so fat it was a second ass.

Where did you find your cheeks after I carved them from your
    face?

You are dead, Amber. I won't believe in you.
Just you try and climb on top of my fridge tonight.
I will soak you in lighter fluid, burn you in a skillet,
then wash it, dry it before it rusts.

Ken

You look nice in that polyester shirt, gleam on your hard chest,
a perfect wave in your hair. You look like an anchorman or politician.

Oh, Ken. You are so dreamy.
You're not too good to help Barbie do inventory.
You're not too pretty to fight Brown Bear
when he throws soup cans on the floor.

But there's something strange playing about your lips.
Someone has drawn a pocket of peach flesh
where there should be teeth.

I see you staring past Barbie. You cannot hold her cupped palm.
You're tired of driving her pink car.

I know you hate stocking those cans of soup, your same white shirt,
and Brown Bear in the alley trying to sober up,
trying to get Barbie to look his way.

Hotel Party

James Dean must be escorted to a hotel party
because that bored look means trouble.
The cigarette is limp on his lips. He'll kill himself.
His eyebrow is fuzzy but I won't smooth it for him.
He smells like my father.

I take him to find Linda from high school,
Linda who squinted and flirted with boys who didn't notice.
I see her frizzy pigtails. She's not so special.
I'm not so special. I, too, wear olive cargo pants.
James Dean hugs her. He's so young. He's so tan.
Linda doesn't squint.

I don't know any James Dean movies. So he's mute
and wearing clothes from a poster.
I can't see him in profile.

Then my husband is coming home. My mother is here to help.
I must scrub the bathtub. Sweep the floor, no AC.
I sweat until my pigtails are fuzzy.
There's no time to ask why the hotel room is now my apartment,
why it seemed I walked for miles to get here.
"This powder smells nice," my mother is saying,
waving a bottle from the bathroom.
I almost slap her hand away.

The floors shine. So does my face.
No time for powder now, my husband is home.
Will he notice all these garbage bags?
Scuff marks on the dining room floor?

Princess Di in an Afterlife

She is in the middling place,
a room of doors layered in rows.
She opens one and finds dresses:
her favorite has a bodice made of butterflies.
They dust her collarbone.

Sometimes she finds whole kingdoms,
sometimes only footraces: barefoot young girls
who run with bees sitting on their necks,
the backs of their loose hands.

The doors contain land mines,
orphans with kernels for eyes,
banquets.

Even in the Afterlife
they don't let you leap down a flight of stairs
to find yourself finished with the body's gospel,
and on to some ordinary heaven,
where grapes and oranges
fountain when bit.
She'd welcome their streams into her eyes,
exchange her salt for their tart,
their sharp, their sweet.

My Brother Receives His Kingdom under a Tree

He is laved by sun, and wind, and a bird's shadow,
its plumage multiplied by leaves.

He prunes roses in the front drive
of a new house. A neighbor watches
standing in her window. He greets her.

His raiment is the freedom of kneeling
on his own soil. A freedom that will grow
like the space between knuckles.

Boy who skipped princehood, and is now kinged
in a grove of half-bloomed bushes,
sun and work heating his shirt so he smells detergent.

Our mother makes the best prayers by sliding doors,
offers extra supplication facing the backyard.
All will restrain their curses or have them catch in throats.

A black man crowned with his Prescription,
unerring, drafted in precision, with order:
what has been gifted is delivered.

His staff is a slender waxy branch
whose tip pierces the veins of leaves.

Arrange them how you will, hold fast with your fist.
Your inheritance is a chest of men's tears, fresh and ancient dirges,
the soles of a woman's feet whose voice reaches the sky.
Yours is a kingdom of Position. And the crown, it extends.

Proud Flesh

Can the stars blossom with artificial light,
further decorate the woman born with earrings?

One earring small and plain, the other wood finely turned,
sisters who are two kinds of beautiful.

I offer her accessory. In this light,
a pomegranate seed rolled against gums can be a ruby.

My pearls are stark moons at the lobe,
but I can remove them, give her buttons at the nape

or press cuff links into the man who stares at her growths.
He must be similarly adorned for her. She is an occasion.

If he lies ear to ear with her, they will hear the ocean,
the sighs between its waves, the whisper in its roar.

The Albatross Holds a Note in Her Bill

Stun her with the bolt your sax makes in this light. Strike her.

Trane refuses, asking, weren't we denied this flesh? I will not,
and goes on playing the song of rebuke,
its harmonies like manna and quail on the ninth night.

Will you deny me? Didn't you follow as I divided a sea for you,
like a curtain, like a blouse?
Will you now fashion a calf out of brass?

Miles smothers the valve keys, Mother-of-Pearl,
and this is the kind of night he cannot forgive
the basket placed in the Nile.

Wasn't I your bugle? Trane plays, the Albatross on his shoulder.
Didn't I help you speak when your tongue was knotted?
And where is the land of milk and honey?

Their blows scream at a silent rock, or the split tabernacle,
or the moon like a good woman walking away,
their hands reaching for her dress and tearing its hem.

I strike you with the abandoned note, adrift beyond the riverbank
because you deserve to feel the pain I feel knowing a spell
that only lifts the Albatross higher and away.

The Trumpet Testifies

and only my mother hears when I say,
I wish I could understand my father.

The surprised note a fist in the middle of my back.
I feel that when you do that to me.

I cut. And I bleed.
It's not always just your water pouring out of me.

Why do you let my body corrode?

When my father oils the valves and stops up the spaces
in which I can holler without him,

it's like the cold knots in heated leftovers.

Italicized speech taken from Michael Jackson quotes.

Following the Horn's Call

Someone labeled a postcard of *The Last Supper*
"People Eating Food."

I laughed because a fish was only fish, bread only bread
until someone explained about Jesus.
In heaven there must be dinners.

If I could get close enough to any honorable table I would say,
"Moses, I had trouble with *r*'s and *s*'s. How about you?
Did God unloose your tongue all at once?"

Do they love Jonah or do they laugh at him?
Do they ask how many arches in the beast's mouth?
Did he count them like ceiling tiles?
Do they say, I trembled when the sea split?
When the flame spoke. When the one who plays the first note
of the last moment showed me his wings.

Do all the women cut their palms because of Joseph's beauty?
Does he ever smile at his own face in the cutlery?
I want to see him and compare him to the others.

Paradise is to ask whatever you like. A tea with God.
I have filled a book with questions I can't remember.

The Beetle

A stink beetle makes tracks on a dune before the sand is warm.
At night the wind moved sand against it like a house full of children
to the front door when a guest comes.

A beetle rests on the prayer house wall.
The women's eyes watch it. Some curse it.
A woman, broom in hand, answers them.

The beetle asks, don't I have a right to this house?
It waits for them to prostrate so it can continue up the wall.

Be a shadow for your Lord, they would hear it say
if their minds were not already crowded.

It is a morning of a thousand months,
the beetle walking where the sand did the night before
on a path similar to the lines on the back of a woman's thigh.

A Dove Sings for Young Lovers

She's a Negro dove
so her song sounds like
a man divining scratch-offs,
false discerner of his own fortunes.
She cups possibility,
puts it in a pocket,
throws it in the garbage,
and purchases another.

Her voice magnifies her body,
a shadow filtered by leaves.

They think that's Soul they're hearing.
But she's too modest to show
both her transcendence and guilt.
Do you know what it feels like to be held
between shame and elevation? This song does.
Soul feels like a dreaded wrapping
or your spirit rising out the top of your head.
This is not Soul.

It's more like a screaming threat, worked to sound like trills.
The song asks, how come they keep wanting me
when they're in heat? Don't they have their own moanings?
Don't they like nothing at all sometimes?

I'm just singing your denigration
for all the times someone thought I was a crow
and didn't listen, though the song was familiar.
I'm just singing oil slicks into your hair.
Listen for your debasement. Don't ask why

you feel so needy when I give you the silhouette
of a piss stain. Don't reach out for that olive branch.
It's already down my throat.
All I got is this match.
Turn the flame on yourselves.

Western Gate

They say women's dreams stay indoors.
These days I dream an ocean under the bed.
I wake up and watch its tide.
I'm myself but also a large black bird,
like the crows near oceans.
I sit up in bed. I perch on the concrete sill.
I'm big enough to slap pavement upon impact,
take running steps to land.
I shout for myself to fly
but only look back at myself
and the water rises
so the whole room smells like salted water
and soaked beans. Have you ever tried to walk
when the water recedes, leaving a chainmail pattern
in the sand, feet sinking? Have you ever
tried to walk watching the water move
and fallen right into it?
The sinking woman will try to make waves
a column, its froth a steady handhold.

I've been having a problem with my eyes.
I keep thinking they'll get paper cuts.
I squint and reveal floaters on every surface.
I could never see past what's right in front of me,
and dislike the whole house if it has broken blinds.
I can't ignore the shapes floating past my retina.
I can't submit. I align them for inspection,
the runs in my humor: Clogged Pipe, Jellyfish, the Titanic.
They grow with each pass.
"Look beyond them," my father would say

when he'd catch me squinting into light, the other eye wide
and rolling, flicking madly to catch any figure.

One night, a black spider in my pillowcase.
"God sent me here to protect you."
"Okay," I said. "Come on in."
"Who are you talking to?" my husband asked.
I told him a spider with the most beautiful voice
would be sleeping with us from now on.
From time to time, I would see her outside,
dangling at the window, her large abdomen
gleaning. At dusk, a katydid at ear-level,
trilling like a transformer. Every sunset,
pray, pray, pray in currents that grate my heart.
But I can't always do it. I hide from it,
from the windows.

Is there a shadow in the dust?
Is there some depression in the dust?
Someone please track the visitant
whose entrance implies a new dimension.
It's as odd as a cat standing before you,
watching you pray. Claws at your forehead.
Pouring skin-temperature water over yourself,
wondering, have I dressed in unseen garments?
Or scripture playing to an empty room.
How long will my second self
jump up and go to the first exit?

After a season of night terrors—
leaves, feathers, lapping water,
men with lights, then torsos of light,
a large bird appeared on the sill.

It was bigger than all the others.
"What do you want?
Should I die so you can
take this bed?"
It looked sad and faced westwards,
eyes jaundiced. So I sat up,
and told it to *leave, leave.*
I flapped my wrists.
It turned from me, facing west.
A breeze lifted a collar of feathers.
I was again it, myself.
By then I was ready to go crazy,
lay my head on the bottom of a tub
filled with my crazy.
And then it flew away
and the torsos and ocean went with it,
and I was myself, again
and peaceful with my three shadows
when walking in any new night.

IN THE AFRICAN POETRY BOOK SERIES

*The Promise of Hope: New and
Selected Poems, 1964–2013*
Kofi Awoonor
Edited and with an introduction
by Kofi Anyidoho

Madman at Kilifi
Clifton Gachagua

*Seven New Generation African
Poets: A Chapbook boxed set*
Edited by Kwame Dawes and Chris Abani

The Kitchen-Dweller's Testimony
Ladan Osman

To order or obtain more information on
these or other University of Nebraska Press
titles, visit www.nebraskapress.unl.edu.

CPSIA information can be obtained
at www.ICGtesting.com
Printed in the USA
LVHW030131181121
703693LV00002B/303